W9-BWW-575

TAKE OFF YOUR BRAVE

The World through the Eyes of a Preschool Poet

Nadim (age 4)

illustrated by Yasmeen Ismail

CANDLEWICK PRESS

INTRODUCTION

by Nadim's mother, Yasmine Shamma

In early 2020, our four-year-old son, Nadim, brought home a poem from preschool. We sat together at the table and we talked about what a poem could be, how poems sometimes rhyme and sometimes don't. This struck Nadim as exciting—what would a poem be without rhyme? Or as he put it, "Is it like a kind of story?" I explained, "It's a kind of story of a feeling, or a moment," and his eyes seemed to dance, imagining the possibilities. Inspired by a poet-friend and colleague who works with children, I asked Nadim to think about the story of the moment of coming home. "What do you take off and put on the table by the front door? Let's make a list," I said, "and see where it goes." When he got stuck after having thought of all the physical things he removes when he comes home, I simply asked, "Anything else?" to which Nadim generously offered, "You take off your brave."

In that moment, the poem became a meaningful place of conversation. Through the form of the poem, Nadim shared his experiences of the world, and offered us an aperture into that world. Poetry also empowered him with the notion that his words and thoughts mattered, and merited being written down on a piece a paper, read back to him, and considered a poem. From then on, making poems became a special kind of play for Nadim to explore with us.

Nadim now reads and writes on his own—he no longer needs me as his Dictaphone—but he still comes to me when he has an idea for a poem; poetry has become a way of talking for us, and I hope it always will be. It could be for other children and their caregivers too. Sit down with your child, take out a piece of paper, grab a pen, and listen. Childhood *is* poetry, and the child who has the attention of their parent or caregiver for a quiet moment will more often than not let the poem inside them out.

This book collects the poems Nadim wrote that first year, as well as poems from Nadim's sister and his preschool class. Its magic is that it offers bright-eyed, fresh renditions of children's poetry, written *by* children *for* children, hopefully encouraging other children to give poetry a try. As Nadim explains, "Anyone can write a poem if they just put on a paper what they think thoughtfully."

My husband and I are both educators, and over the years we've found Nadim's words to be true. Whether we're sitting down with our own four-year-old, a group of ten-year-olds, or a class of twenty-year-olds, the biggest challenge in understanding and writing poetry is overcoming the notion of tradition—that a poem should sound a certain way, that it should follow certain strictures. It *can*, and this can enact its own formula of beauty, but it doesn't have to. A different magic unfolds when you tell a child: a poem is what you want it to be—don't worry about what you think a poem *should* be. "Should" gestures toward a voice from outside of you. "Want" comes from inside—the place where "brave" may be born.

Love

Everyone has to love someone
Flamingos loves someone
The wind loves someone
The sea loves someone
Spirits
Letters
Houses
Everything you ever know loves someone

Everyone has love
Even baddies

My Dream School

All the kids turn into kittens

when they get into the dream school.

There will be no bullies

And the teachers are all friendly dinosaurs

And all they do is chat chat chat

with anyone they want.

The school smells like daffodils, honey,

And sometimes stinky socks.

(Some people faint when it smells like stinky socks.)

The kids are always making cardboard teleporters

But the grown-ups just sew toys.

Everyone loves that school.

Miss Angela

by Nadim and his sister, Taleen,
written to their old preschool teacher

Miss Angela is nice.
Miss Angela smells like flowers.
Miss Angela smells warm.
Miss Angela sounds like a bell, ringing gently.

It makes me sad
that we're not going
to get to see
Miss Angela
every day
anymore.

Bluebell, Where Did You Get Your Blue?

by Nadim's preschool class

Bluebell, where did you get your purply blue?
Did you get your blue from the sea?
Did you get your purple from a purple butterfly?
Maybe the butterfly gave the bluebell a kiss?
Where did you get the green of your stem?
Did you get it from the grass?
Did you get it from a playset?
No, definitely not from a playset.
Did you get the green of your stem from a leaf?
And where did you get your bluebell smell?
Did you get it from the sunshine?
Did you eat the sunlight up?
You smell like blueberries. And glitter.
And butterflies fluttering around.

Being on a Train

Feels like *bumpity bump*

Sounds like *chuka chuka shhhhh*

Smells a bit like air and eating smells

Mostly sandwiches

It looks like being on a very giant long car

But it goes a bit faster

Goes to lots of cities and even countries

And is really bumpy

There's all these different stops

And stop   stops are really different

Because it's like you're on a giant bus

Because they're in the same country

In a train you think about anything really

Sometimes you can think about it as floating

Or living in a monster's tummy

Because it feels really movable in a train

In a train you dream about anything really

Like floating in a bubble in your home

Sometimes you could be walking in a train

Looking for the time or your home or anything you want to see

Like the moon

Or a magic bus

My Best Friend

Eddie is not calm.
Eddie is fast.

He's as fast as anyone—
Faster than everyone—
Faster than anyone
And everyone you've ever seen.
And he knows pretty much everything
About aliens.

He lives near my old school in a house
(it's made of bricks and it looks really cool)
And it always has an orange flag outside
    And bikes
    And flowers
And there are always snacks at his house
And he shares his toys
(they're really cool)
And we play.

Tell Me About a Day of the Week

Wednesday is rainbow-colored,
Because it's got all the colors in the world—
Because it's so lovely.

Wednesday's loveliness
Comes from the earth
And smells like roses.
And Wednesday wears a shirt with glitter on it.

Tell Me a Lie About the Sea

The sea doesn't have any waves.
It doesn't make a sound.
The fish make the *shhhh* sound.
The seaweed doesn't have any names,
And it makes the *shhhh* sound too.

In the sea without sound,
The manatee finds its bed
In the coral reef
With the Nemo fish.
It snuggles up tight
In its beautiful coral bed and
Snugs to go to sleep. It's easy for it to fall asleep
In the sea without waves and sound.

shhhh
sh h hh h h
shhhhh
shhhh
z z z z z z z z z
shh h h
shhh
sh
shh
shhhh
shhh

Little

by Nadim's sister, Taleen

This is a poem by my cute little pony. She's called Little.

Because I've been reading,
learning, sleeping, and eating.
And I've also been hugging and snuggling.
And I've also been loving my parents, my whole life.
And I've also been playing with my best friends.
And I've also been getting treats
like vitamin gummies and ice cream
and my things I wish for.
And I've also been exploring.
So I have learned so much,
during this holiday and in general.

Baddies

Baddies love their baddie friends
Even very baddie ones.

Nothing can make love disappear
Not spells
Not magic
Not mermaids
Not anything.

People might have rough moments
They might have sad moments
They might have shocked moments
They might have scared moments
They might have crackled moments
They might have unhappy moments
They might have really bad moments
But their love won't disappear.

Love in baddies

Love in good, protective people

Love in animals

Love in windstorms

Love in penguins

Love in baddies, too.

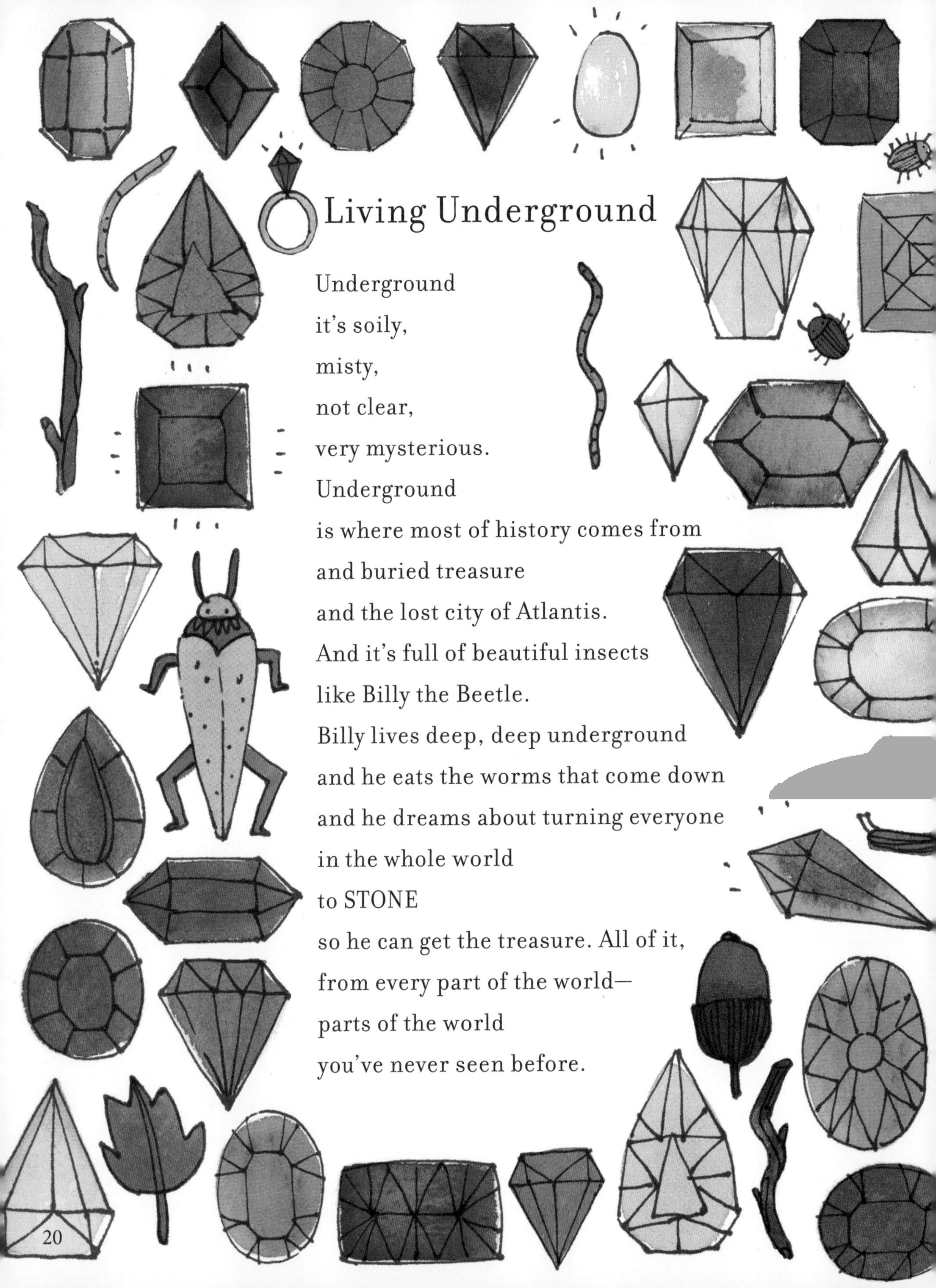

Living Underground

Underground
it's soily,
misty,
not clear,
very mysterious.
Underground
is where most of history comes from
and buried treasure
and the lost city of Atlantis.
And it's full of beautiful insects
like Billy the Beetle.
Billy lives deep, deep underground
and he eats the worms that come down
and he dreams about turning everyone
in the whole world
to STONE
so he can get the treasure. All of it,
from every part of the world—
parts of the world
you've never seen before.

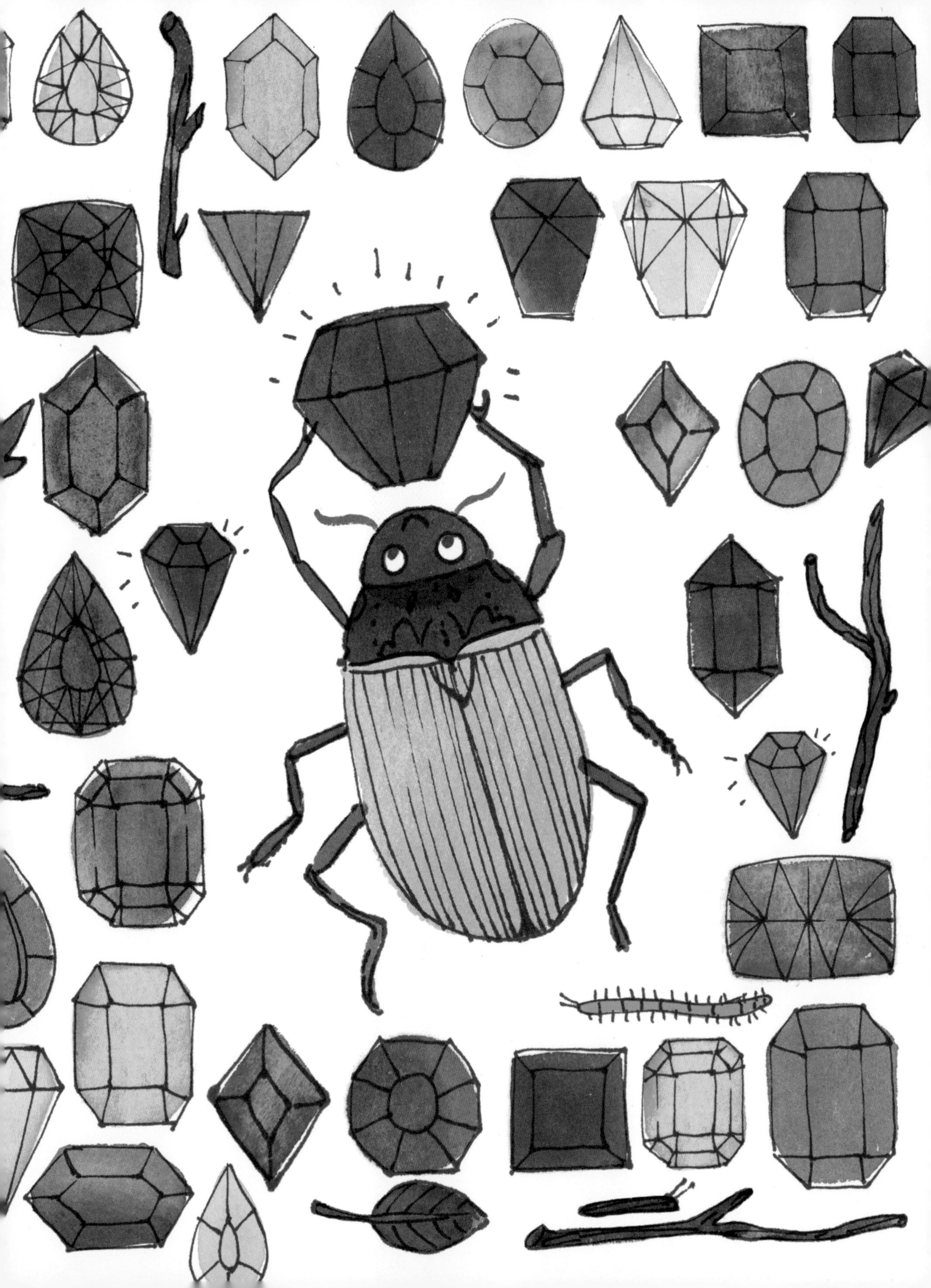

The Busy Cat

by Nadim's preschool class

The busy cat wears ginger fur—
It wears a black fluffy hat.
The busy cat is eating lunch:
The busy cat eats tuna
And sometimes a salad with fish.
(The busy cat eats cat biscuits too.)
The busy cat waits for it to snow
So he can make snow-cat angels.

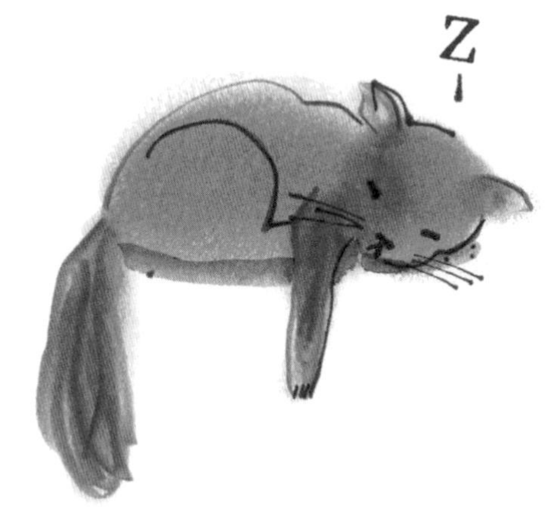

The busy cat smells like ginger—
It also smells like hope.
The busy cat hopes for a friend:
The busy cat's best friend will be a brave cat.
The busy cat's favorite time of day
    is naptime
When it puts on its sleeping cat
And it takes its little catnap.

Oh! My Best Things

Oh, owls!
Oh, playing with my sister, my whole family!
(Even if it's the whole big one
It's still my favorite.)

Watching William play football
outside the garden window.
Playing with Daddy.
The smell of baked things.
I love love.
I love my family extra much.

Oh, glitter, Legos, books!
Looking at wood lice and bugs,
Eating ice cream,
And snuggling
With you.

Memories

Sometimes, when I look at my memories
It makes me a bit sad—
Like when I'm at a different stage
It makes me think, "Oh . . .
I'm never going to get to do that again."

Mom, did you ever have that feeling?
Like when you went to school
And then it ended
And you started another one?

Magic Box

This box is for you, Auntie.
Covered in rainbow-glittered stars,
Filled up with lots of roses
And apples and oranges
So if you're hungry
You could just take one out
To snack on.

I'll put some secret toy elves in there
To play with, if you're bored—
They're electrical.
You can wind them up with a key in their back
That can make them talk or walk.

I'll put in the box
A baby moon
And pictures of smiley faces
That really smile.

I'll just close the lid
And wrap it
And send it with a magic spell
To you—
Even if you're just next to me,
Like right now.

Magic Box

by Nadim's sister, Taleen

I'm going to send my magical box to Olivia.
I would put some magic pink stars in it
And Olivia will open them
And sparkly shiny things will glitter up.
I would send her a unicorn toy:
An Olivia toy.
(I wouldn't send my Unicorn
Who married Owly yesterday.)

I would send Olivia the moon.
I would send Olivia food.
I already sent her a lot of things—
And a hug.

My Lonely Garden

It’s peaceful:
Calm.
Especially when
There are bugs flying around in the sun
And I get to just be thinking
On my nice blue bench
And all I can feel on my back is sunshine
And all I get to do is look at the beautiful plants and things
And do whatever I want
In my garden.

Moments

You always have sad moments
Happy moments
Nice moments
Angry moments

And when you smush those moments together
They make a great feeling
Called:
ABRACADABRACDOCUOUS.

For My Mom

Who was the one who feeds me mostly?
It's my mom, it's my mom.
Who's the one that bathes me mostly?
It's my mom, it's my mom.
Who's the one who gives me snuggles?
It's my mom, it's my mom.

She's the one who does me airplane.
She's the one who takes me to nursery school.
She's the one who takes me from Lunch Club.
She's the one who goes to work in the world,
  for me.

You smell like a beautiful candle smell.
You smell like a candle when it blows away.
It smells really nice—the burnt bit.
You smell like a blown candle.

Take Off Your Brave

Take off our jackets
Hang them up

Take our gloves off
Take our shoes off
Put them where
They're supposed to go

You take off your brave feeling

Because there's nothing
To be scared of in the house:
No dark caves no monsters
No witches no bees no howling sounds

You don't need your brave anymore

Wash your hands

Eat lunch

Go get cozy.

Scared-Sugar

Did you ever have that feeling
That you were scared about doing something kind of scary,
But it was also kind of sweet?
Like the first time you meet new friends
Like touching a sea anemone
Like sleeping over at your cousin's house
Like eating a new food
Like becoming 5 instead of 4
Like saying bye to your mom
When you go to a new school.

You would feel nervous but excited
And that's a feeling called scared-sugar.

For scared-sugar things, you put on your brave
And you can take it off again, when you realize it's OK.
And that's it. Scary and sweet. Scared-sugar.

Between Bathtime and Bedtime

Can you get muscles in your muscles?
What does a cloud feel like?
What are all the fishes' names?
And what are all the animals called?
How much types of leopards are there?
What are all the names in the world?
Can you get muscles in your lungs?
Does everyone know what the moon feels like?
What do fire ants taste like?
How much types of gadgets are there?
What are all the parts of your body for?
What are birthmarks for?
How do they appear?
Is there any man on the moon?
Why are roosters important?
Does anything eat humans?
How did the world appear?
Is God actually real?
How much stars are there in the world?
Everyone loves poems.
How are bubbles made?
How do light bulbs get their light?
I know that all of these questions are real
And poems are too.

?
?
?
?
?
?
?
?
?
?
?
?
?
click!
Z

My Wish

Was that we lived on a different planet
That was calm and quiet
With no countries or cities
Just a whole big town
That wasn't so busy
With lots of cafés and shops
And everyone was magical
Because whenever they moved their fingers
And said something they really wanted to happen
It would just come true very quickly

And on that planet
There were no deep craters
And there were beautiful flowers in all the seasons
Even winter
And lots of friendly and nice beautiful birds
And lots of them are robins
And lots of beautiful beaches
With lots of pearls and seashells
And lots of warm weather on the planet.
And lots of love.
And . . .

THE END.

For my mom
N

With love for Alasdair, Ted, and Fara
YI

Grateful acknowledgment is given that the poem on page 8 was written using a prompt inspired by Kenneth Koch's wonderful book *Rose, Where Did You Get That Red?* (Vintage, 1990).

First US edition 2022
First published by Walker Books (UK) 2021

Library of Congress Catalog Card Number 2021946646
ISBN 978-1-5362-2316-3

21 22 23 24 25 26 APS 10 9 8 7 6 5 4 3 2 1

Printed in Humen, Dongguan, China

This book was typeset in Filosofia.
The illustrations were done in mixed media.

Candlewick Press
99 Dover Street
Somerville, Massachusetts 02144

www.candlewick.com